FOR ONE WHO KNOWS HOW TO OWN LAND

by

SCOTT OWENS

FutureCycle Press

www.futurecycle.org

For One Who Knows How to Own Land

Published by FutureCycle Press
Mineral Bluff, Georgia, U.S.A.

ISBN: 978-0-9839985-3-2

for Otis Horace Harvley,
my grandfather

Contents

LEANING THROUGH DARKNESS

THE UNDISCOVERED COUNTRY

TO RESIST FADING

LEANING THROUGH DARKNESS

Between the Rails

He found God between two cars
of the line from Greenwood to Clinton,
where his feet had frozen in place
on the small block holding the coupler.
His hand still held the ladder rung
he had swung down from
and could easily climb again
if only his feet would move.

He stood trembling between them,
watching the couplers push and pull
each other like locked jaws of dogs
fighting, watching the one hose
swell and breathe with the back
and forth pulling, the rough bed
shaking, the rocks pushing into the rails.

He heard the screaming of wheels
against rails, the pulsing at bolted
joints, the banging and groaning
of huge bodies against each other,
struggling it seemed
to come together or fall apart.

When he looked up he saw the face
twisted before him, the eyes
clenched shut, the mouth a perfect
O. He felt the breath hot
and loud around him, tasted
the sweat, smelled the odor

like wet leaves. The open mouth
screamed. The eyes flew open,
pierced him with anger, struck him
like a fist in his chest, taking
his breath away, holding him
tight against the back of the car.

The railroad people called his parents
from Clinton, and his father came to get him,
slapping him all the way home, shouting
about closed doors, groundings, railroads,
repeating never again, never again.
Afterwards it would always seem the same,
the hardened features, the stony eyes,
the fleeting images trapped between the rails,
the fist beating in his chest.

Breakings

There were always bottles in the well house,
lined up on 2 X 4s, piled in boxes, hidden
above the door. He hung them, bottoms up,
on the sticks he planted in the pasture.
Sometimes he used coffee cans, milk jugs,
a red-lined slopjar, anything to make a noise
as it swallowed the rocks or took the blows
hard against its side. But nothing could match
the sounds of shattered glass, nothing
could match the thrill of breaking.

The changes came sudden but incomplete.
What was once a bottle grew into
the many faces of breaking,
mirrors and windows, stung
running of cows, frantic beating
of redbirds, cries of children.

His father went off to war
to practice breaking on other men.
He became so good at it he came back
to teach others the black magic of breaking.

His mother stayed home and broke water,
broke in husbands and children,
broke her back to hold
some fragment of family together.

The old man, his grandfather,
broke the earth, broke cows

in the pasture, chicken-bones
in his teeth, taught him to break
limbs with the red axe,
the necks of chickens and rabbits,
legs of owls in foxtraps,
skulls of cows in the stable.

He saw the breaking of land,
the endless bending of backs
and knees, the big-handed breaking
of his mother's face, his brother's
mouth, his own shattered skin.
He saw the black eyes of ants
shining as he snapped off their legs,
felt limbs give way beneath his weight
and smiled to think it all
could end this way.

He heard the news of breaking,
of Attica and Kent, King
and My Lai, the fields and jungles
scattered with war, the streets
emptied through breaking of walls
and windows, hearts and heads.

He saw the night shattered
with noise and lights, a man's body
broken open on the porch
the life splattered on the window,
lying messy on the floor.

He wanted to leave it all
behind, to break the habits
of breaking, but even now,
he knows the hearts of those
he loves like glass.

Leaning Through Darkness to See the Stars

B-B's would only wound them,
poke holes in their wings,
shake loose a feather or two,
unless you caught them in the eye,
a rare shot, more luck than skill.
Slingshots did more damage,
though much of it less visible,
but still rarely killed them right away.
Sometimes you could watch them fly
a few hundred feet before falling,
then find them on the ground, panting,
flapping a last good wing,
the black coat, black eye,
streaked with constellations of red.
Shotguns made short work of it,
but ruined the bodies,
and scared the others away for hours.

Summers we picked them off
as they rose or settled among the corn,
dark spots in the green day.
In autumn we shot them out of tree tops,
dark bodies filling the sky
like a single great wing.

Wherever there was corn it was necessary
Straw men did little to frighten
their number. Once every single man
was required to kill a dozen
and not allowed to marry until he had done so.

Most seemed half-dead already, wings
tattered and pocked full of holes,
faces sloppy and scarred.
Only their eyes seemed clear,
black stones shining in death's dull face.

The Event Rightfully Remembered

The white horse
whose hoof slipped
between the boards
of our makeshift bridge
could have been
a white Pinto
whose drunken tire
slid off the edge,
a birch branch blown
between the boards
in a summer storm,
or the white horse
whose hoof slipped
between the boards
of our makeshift bridge.

The redness spraying
the old man's face
as he pulled it from the trap
of wood and nails
could have been
the sun reflected
in the rearview mirror,
the mud running
down the driveway,
or the blood surging
from the broken leg.

The redness in the old
man's hands as he dragged

16

the skin to the pit
of wood and ash
could have been
flakes of rust
from an old wheel,
tree sap bleeding
from the wounded branch,
blood stains clinging
to wrinkled palms,
or just the color
of an old man's
furrowed hands
that handled life
and death like two ends
of the same season.
Anything else
would have been
too weak to survive
all these years
in the mind of a boy
too young to understand.

7 Haiku

bright morning
after three days of spring rain—
everything opens

          screen door
          hum of cicada
          as if heat could sing

wildflowers in bloom
the tractor stops a moment
then plows them under

          tractors sow the field
          into one fabric
          dream of green leaves

all day heat lightning
flashes on the horizon
still no rain

          grandfather
          strops the much-stropped edge
          racing blowflies

yellow porch light
illuminating darkness
swirl of candle bats

Americana

We arrive again, at night,
nearly as hot as it is in the day.
Candle bats swarm the yellow
porch light. The old woman,
wrapped in flowered gowns,
smelling of Vicks, helps us in.
You wouldn't call her crazy yet,
though we've all seen the signs.

Mama carries one, then another,
puts them both in one bed
in the back room, box fan blowing
summer's heat around, thin curtain
moving with night sounds coming in.
She takes the other. My brother and I
lay down pallets, pile blankets
and quilts high enough to sink into,
ask for a spoonful of ice milk
to help hold off the heat.

The old man already sleeps and dreams
of 4 A.M., tending cows
before leaving for the quarry. It's hard
to know what was left this time,
another man, another house
unafforded, another time trying to solve
the final equations of leaving.

Feeding Time

Red ice cracks
beneath black boots
walking across the dung field.
White-faced calves
slide against each other,
low for the false tit,
white breath forming circles
around their heads.

The old cow follows him
to the feedhouse, stumbles
through the crumbled door.
His hand stretches across
her white face, gently
strokes her red neck,
rubs the bulging ribs,
squeezes the cold tit.

He moves the bucket aside,
ties the lead to the trough
where he pours the grain,
and quietly steps outside.
He fingers the knot-hole
above the trough, slowly
inserts the barrel
and waits.

When the feeding is finished
he notices the warm smell
of her coat on his, red ice

moving around his boots,
smoke circling the barrel,
fat calves running
like frightened children
over frozen pastures.

Dowry

Before the light,
the whippoorwill wakens,
sings in dark trees,
around the house,
among the leaves,
over the roofs of the farm.
He calls from black limbs
poor Jack rising to the edge
of the dark, rising
to the edge of the trees
thick with the thousand
sounds of clicking
grasshoppers still
heavy with dew.

The purple sky
dissolves into blue.
The whippoorwill fades
into meadowlark.
The young woman, awake
and alone in the narrow
bed, stretches stiffly,
rubs her crusted eyes,
touches her aching stomach,
listens to him
calling in the pasture
and fat calves
bellowing in return.

She lies in bed awhile
until she hears him
in the yard, amid
the cackle of hens
and baby chicks,
a man whose hands
could as easily bring
life as take it away.
She rises slowly,
brushes back her hair,
walks to the bathroom
for her daily cleansing.
In the kitchen she lights
a fire beneath the pot,
sets the water to boil,
prepares his toast and eggs,
and waits for the distant
sound of his boots banging
on the step, shaking
loose the morning mud.

Slaughter

I only saw his face in butchery once,
the dumb, dead beast hung
from a hickory tree, legs spread,
tendons split, the rusted rack
draped with skin, dripping bone.

I'd seen him twist heads
off chickens, shed skin of rabbits,
batter skulls of fox, hawk, possum,
but nothing made a space in memory
like this reduction of life so large.

When did he get rid of the head?
I was there when he fired the single shot
through the knothole, the beast tied inside
to its last trough. I was there
when the big knife sliced across the red-

brown throat, when the feet stopped kicking.
I was there when the chain clicked and strained
against the canvas weight, hauling
it up, inverted, Christ-like, neck
an empty sleeve. How could I miss

his taking the head off, among the blood
and smell, the peeled-back skin,
the silent, serious faces,
among the brown and purple lungs,
the dogs lapping everywhere?

Whippoorwills call unseen,
candlebats fly crazy patterns into night,
and the old man carves flesh streaked red
as stone, hands cracked, eyes
like stars, face a circle of darkness.

My Grandfather's Hands

were always covered with the stuff,
the red dirt of earth he knew as his own,
the etched-in reminders of everything
he touched: white globes of onions,
red bags of tomatoes, yellow veins
of quartz. All day he spent with his hands
in the earth, digging in the quarry,
digging in the garden. Each night he tried
to take it off, turning his hands
like soil in the sink, scrubbing
the furrows of fingers, scraping
the hard mounds of his palms.

No matter how much he removed
there was always more, caked beneath
the fingernails, packed in the cracks
of his hands, the smell of onions
rising, his touch growing harder,
his motions more like digging each day.

Preserving the Horn

Rings of convoluted age expand outward
from the severed root, each layer growing
on top of the last, thickening as it stretches
to the pale tip, an old scar graying
in naked air.

A single dark vein running from root
to tip throbs beneath the wash of lather
up and back, hardens beneath rough hands,
seems still to carry blood
to fading cells.

The ribbed root, cut in youth,
regrew in storied rings, is now
reduced to this slick souvenir,
bleached and sterilized, hanging limp
in wrinkled hands.

All Summer Long the Rain

waited beyond the mountains,
refused to fall here
where it was most needed.
Flowers faded and died.
Grass and skin browned
with burning. Farmers plowed
and replowed the same land,
dust running behind them
like horses. Houses grew dull
and tired, crouched ever closer
to the ground. Creeks refused
to speak their words of running.

After six weeks without rain
wells began to run dry.
After eight weeks we set up
altars to the sky, barrels open
on top, willow branches
stuck two prongs in the ground.

After ten weeks Willie Brooks
rode over the mountains
to see what kept the rain,
but came back empty and unsure.

Now we stand in doorways, watching
the sky, our lips dry and hard
as hands, no one saying anything
but "When it comes. When it comes."

Fixing the Lines

Twisted wire wedged in the crotch
of the pry bar, I lean back,
press the iron neck against the post,
pull the line tight for fastening.
My uncle strikes the staple three times,
its teeth biting deep in old wood.
All around us red cows stretch long
necks across the cutting strands
of barbed wire. Between them we see
the road's red bank, black turn,
green border of clover and weed.
The air is filled with autumn,
with things fallen. There is a sadness
in the way my uncle taps the staple home,
his gloved hand like something trapped
between the lines. With every stroke
of the hammer the cows raise their heads,
look for a moment, then bend their necks
again, certain life on the other side
is better, sweeter, purer,
unsoiled by their own manure.

Holding On

This last living vine cuts into my hand,
pulls a thin line of blood from brown
fingers, struggles against separation.
I pull harder, stumble, almost fall when it breaks
spraying the ground with a rattle of dry leaves.

Once a secret hiding place, the matted vines
could be raised like a blanket. A child hidden
underneath became lost in the musky smell,
the happy tongues of scuppernong.

Today the bushaxe tears until nothing remains
but a frayed stump we wrap with chains for pulling.
The tractor, started, bucks, heaves, belches smoke
from a rusted muffler. The ground swells,
cracks, but will not open. The stump breaks,
but remains rooted. The chain flies free,
clatters at the tractor's feet. What's left
is wrapped again, the struggle renewed.
The earth rises like bread, the wood seems certain
to give, but then the chain breaks,
rushes at the tractor like a mad dog, spitting
and snapping, fleeing a gnarly stump too deeply
rooted, too much alive beneath the ground.

Coming to the Surface

CAT-capped heads bowed beneath
the hot shade of broad tobacco leaves
rush to the end of long rows, leave
behind the skeleton stalks of summer.
Today, like no other, no one stops
to collect arrowheads or smoke
a loosely rolled joint. As one, we hurry
towards noon, helping each other finish
the rows together, then ride the tractors
to the river, where Joe Moses,
the best swimmer in three counties,
will dive for the bottom of Thompson's Hole.

A black hole in the rocky river blasted
by Old Man Thompson in a spell of drunken
foolishness, no one has ever reached
the bottom where the body must have settled.
Many have gone down,
always coming back empty-handed.

At noon, covered with sweat and tobacco gum,
clutching coke bottles filled with salty
nuts, we gather by the swimming hole.
Old shoes plagued with beggar lice
are left in a pile by a twisted stump;
dirty clothes are hung on branches
or laid out on boulders to dry.
Loading his pockets with rocks, Joe climbs
the cheap-jack platform alone,
and wraps long legs around the knotted

rope we'd all swung from, throwing
grimy bodies into cool dark water.
He shimmies hand over hand to where
it's tied off on a thick branch
and climbs dark limbs to the very top.

He stretches to his full height, holding
an uncertain branch above his head,
the sunlight in the tree tops setting
his body on fire,
and then, he drops,
long and straight
back to earth.

The river swallows him beneath
black waters, sucking in the splash
like a closed door. We grow silent,
waiting. If anyone speaks
it is only in whispers.

We watch the surface, stilled with fear,
waiting for a ripple. At last a string
of bubbles tells us he's still there,
but then the water grows thick again
and everything falls silent.

Two minutes
and still no sign
of surfacing.
Suddenly,
somebody jumps in,
flailing his arms beneath the surface.

Soon we all join him, searching
with bare legs in small circles,
making quick dives into the creek,
but never daring too deep.
Someone runs for help,
and then he appears,
breaking through the surface
in a burst of brown skin
and white water, his face
sucking dry air, red clay
dripping like blood
between raised fingers.

For One Who Knows How to Own Land

Night stretches gray
fingers from pine woods.
Yellow tops fall
beneath the long knife.
The old man's denim cap
appears and disappears
behind rows of corn.
Coming closer he strokes
the necks of calves chewing
the tops in his hand,
quiets the barking dogs
with a quick command,
leads the cows to stable.
His calm voice calls
white chickens to roost,
settling on trees and
housetops like shadows,
and then, when all
is still his black boots,
caked with the red day,
bring in the night.

From crooked roads
I see the lights
of porches come on.
I see the houses
holding the sky
and earth apart.
I see the darkness
waiting at the doors,

as if the fields and fences
don't know enough
to stop coming in.
And I realize
those who know how
to own land never rest.
They can always be seen
sitting on ruined porches,
framed in darkness,
deep in the night.

THE UNDISCOVERED COUNTRY

Driving Home from the Hospital

three egrets fly up from a field
near no water, white bodies rising
from earth's furrowed darkness.

The Undiscovered Country

The crooked road runs
like a black river
by red banks.
Two houses, one hollow,
bent on one knee,
sinking into its own foundation,
the other somewhat newer,
though covered with a skin
of red dust, stand
behind an unplowed field
sown with white stones
and gutted skeletons of cars
half-buried in years
of uncut weeds.

Red ruts and black ash
cover the garden.
Briers and blackberry bushes
thread thickened pastures
where cattle and generations
have grown and died.

A wooden barrel,
an old stove,
a new washing machine,
and the front seat of a Bel Air
sit on the porch,
waiting for the wood
to weaken.

In the house an old woman
marks the passing.
Her furrowed hands
reach inside a black stove
and light a fire
to warm the morning.

Regret

Trailers and streetlights,
rattle of crickets,
whippoorwills'
lure of darkness.

Handfuls of moon
spill out on cut grass.
Rough stars
poke holes

in a perfect blanket of sky.
All the words
I never said
thicken the walls

of my mouth.
Circles gather in stone,
circles and lines
beneath a shock of flowers.

What Comes Next

Quiet.
Remembered places.
Phenix City, Greenville,
Wilmington, Bond Street.
The blackbird silent on the fence.
Your body at rest,
at last, in one place.
Your soul in every place
you've ever been,
in every mind
you've ever touched,
still waiting
for quiet.

Moccasins

I should have thanked him for the shoes,
my moccasins, that made me fly,
that kept my feet from touching
the ground, that led me
through spaces between raindrops.
Brown as mud, as the water
he came from, wrinkled, large,
soft as his hands and face,
scarred, scratched, thick
it seemed with dirt or years,
textured leather skin,
smell of cigarettes and animals.

I didn't come the third time
he died, the final time.
I didn't sit by the bed
and hold his hand, wipe
the sweat from his eyes.
I sat in a window instead
watching a sky I remember
from flat land, from pecan trees,
from between rows of corn.
I remembered his mouth and eyes,
his satisfied grin.
I remembered his voice held back,
his laughter, his way of giving
what he never had himself.
I remembered corn stalks stripped
and fed to cows, tomatoes

bigger than two fists, beans
we snapped past nightfall.

Soft, his smile, his touch,
soft as good leather his way
of saying you'd done wrong
or right, soft the memory
of a house, a land, a life
he seemed to hold in hands
too big for holding still.

Triptych

Morning Requiem

The houses are quiet
beneath the veil of morning.
Thick scent of cut grass
climbs the air coming alive
with startling speech
of iridescent birds,
clicking tongues,
rolling r's.
Somewhere a church bell
counts the hours,
an alarm clock calls
and no one answers.

Ascendance

Steam rises from morning
fields like ghosts
of what has been planted.
The smell of newmown hay
greets the day's rising.
A meadowlark calls
from a brown fencepost,
black collar shining
against yellow field.
Somewhere a door opens,
seed clatters in a metal bucket
ready for planting.

Succession

Still cold smell of morning
hangs heavy on the mountain.
Trembling leaves open
their hands to the light,
invite the day's coming,
shake off the color of night
fading into earth. Somewhere
a woodthrush, hidden
among blossoming dogwoods,
sends up his song, resounding
through field and village
and a million years of mountain.

Rosemary is for Remembrance

for my grandfather

Memory is always
the last to go,
waiting for the passing
of voices and words,
the selling or throwing away
of clothes and boxes of goods,
waiting for pictures to fade,
faces to change,
dates to be forgotten.

I missed your funeral
and I never visit your grave,
but when I go home
I pull weeds from your garden
and plant them by the steps
to your house.

I remember your face
was not made of stone,
and your hands were nothing
like angels.

Now

Now there are all these figs
split open on sagging limbs,
pecans rotting on the ground,
fences falling down beneath
blackberries' unchecked growth.

Now the houses are heavy
with themselves. The weight of years
pushes them in like boxes left empty.
Now the boards of roof and floor
hang low, bend towards the ground.

Once so easy to find,
playing hide and seek
in fields of fescue, coming in
with hair black and full
and tangled with grass, twig,

a misplaced feather or two,
they hide much better now,
disappearing into deeper grasses,
lying in flowered beds,
slowly rolling to stone.

Ghost House

The green house still stands,
bent to one knee beneath
a load of forgotten furniture,
rotting potatoes, abandoned toys
and a scrawny litter of unnamed cats.
Green shingles rot and fall,
disappear beneath wet leaves
creeping over the footing.
The chimney stands like a headstone
chiseled where limbs have chipped
at weakening block.
The thick door hangs open
above a fallen porch, leans
towards stone steps
that dead end in mid air.

Something still lives in these walls,
watches from shattered windows,
flees when glimpsed from corners
of eyes, shadows without sources
playing unfinished
games of hide and seek,
stirring ashes in empty stoves,
rattling rusted bedframes,
tromping through hollow halls
until I stop
        silence.

Carcasses

My grandfather's pastures were always filled
with the rusted hulks, shucked-out shells
of automobiles sprawled across the fields,
tireless wheels trapped in tracks
that still held the shapes of passing.
Packards and Hudsons, Falcons and Bel Airs,
broken down Mustangs and Chevys,
they became a part of the landscape, piled
like mounds of earth or huge boulders
the cows could rub their necks against.

Today, only a milk truck remains,
still shielding rotting straw.
The others have disappeared one
by one, some hauled off to junkyards,
others reduced by rain and salvage
to nameless piles of parts, still others
wholly lost beneath the unchecked growth
of goat's rue and fescue, as if the earth,
tired of supporting useless frames,
destroyed the bonds of nut and bolt,
brought down what ran across it,
reclaimed these bared remains.

Skeleton

The burnt chimney rises over the wreck,
blessed with the luck of building saints,
the ancient names of cornerstones.
Riprap like burnt coals holds
black boards sucked dry and moaning,
pulling out their own nails,
their secret shafts shining in cinders.
Dust dances on what remains,
faint hands touching distended arms
of wood that reach for absent ceilings,
fallen floors, remembered walls.

The skeleton sits at the crossroad,
innards exposed, split and shucked,
but still clinging to scorched earth.
Black limbs lean like Andrew's cross,
a single white finger extended,
stabbing into air thick with falling.
Stumps of walls, lampblack and jagged,
squat like old men around the ashes
of the past. The wind moans and raises
nothing but dust from what has been.

My Granny's House

My granny's house was always dark
and never clean though she worked
from sunup to sundown at one thing
or another, baking bread, straining
milk, churning butter. Only for her soaps
would she sit down in a bare recliner,
a bowl of beans in her lap, snapping
and stringing, proclaiming each new
woman saint or whore and saying
men couldn't help their ways.
When my mother turned 14 she told her
to marry since she was bound to sin anyway.

There were always Bibles in my granny's house
and hymns being hummed in the kitchen
though she never went to church and said,
"They's mostly hypocrites that do —
sin all week and think to clear
their conscience by going to church on Sunday."
There were always holes in the floor, and urine
in the toilet she wouldn't flush to save water.
There were bread bags cleaned out for leftovers,
feed bags in trashcans, jelly jars for glasses,
and the slanted dining room built on
to an unfinished Jim Walter 4-room home
bought when the old house started falling in.

There was always red dust from the quarry
and the asphalt plant, pecans bagged
on the porch, tomatoes rotting in windowsills,

the smell of spilled milk and the sweetest butter
I've ever tasted. There was never any
noise but what my granny made
yelling boys out of the house
and the slap of hickory switches on bare legs.

My Papa wasn't there much, up at dawn
to go to the quarry, back at noon,
tending cows and corn, sitting
only to watch the weather before
the sun went down. "A good man,"
she'd say, "a hard worker. Never
hit me, though I know he drank,
and fought the chickens and chased
women around in his younger days.

There were pictures on every wall
of my Granny's house, children and grandchildren,
crosses and Baby Jesus, and the echo
of shouted prayers more frightening
than the first tornado that knocked down the barn
or the second that came right up to her house
and lifted and set down again on the other side,
showing everyone, "Just what kind of Christian" she was.

Pulling the Nails

By then, they had to have had doubts.
The sky had been dark for hours;
the earth had shaken;
saints had risen and been seen.
They must have been uncertain
about touching what remained,
afraid of how it could change them.

Taking down the old house,
I remember leaning forward
on the pry bar, pushing my weight
down, one, two,
three times to get rusted nails
to let go of wood
swollen tight with age,
and when they finally popped out,
I was surprised to see
the light from inside shine through.

I can't help but wonder,
when soldiers pulled the nails
from Christ's hands and feet,
what force had to be used,
if they resisted like this,
and how much light spilled out.

Buzzard

Always
when you look up
at white clouds, blue sky

you see
that hyphen of a bird,
not flying but floating,

silently
keeping two worlds
you imagine apart, together.

TO RESIST FADING

Dirt Farmer

We never had a mule on my Papa's farm
though we had every other kind of creature
a farm in the Piedmont might have, horses
and cows, pigs and goats, chickens,
rabbits, even guinea hens for a while,
and though my Granny and Papa called
each other *Mule* often enough
and worked like mules and often seemed
like mules, not quite one thing or the other,
and though the farm was only a few
miles from the Promised Land where
the government gave every freed slave
an acre and a mule though they never
gave my Papa's daddy nothing
though he was as poor as the poorest
Negro, dirt poor they said, meaning
the floors of his house were dirt, meaning
that in the roughest times he might
have eaten dirt, meaning the color
of his hands and feet and face were the same
as the dirt he worked in, walked on, lived in.
Probably just a way to say
We're sorry though as for that
it seemed a pretty poor apology,
expecting dignity to be returned
through either end of a mule.

To Resist Fading

*from Walker Evans' photograph "Bud Field
and His Family"*

Who can keep them from fading
into walls, floors, their bare feet,
bare shoulders as unwashed
as where they move, their clothes
older than their bodies, worn
like skins that can't be changed.

Who can keep them from disappearing
beneath the roof's falling in,
the walls leaning in at odd angles.
The man's arms are all but given out,
given up, his hands too big
to handle the youngest sleeping heavy
in his mother's lap, her face
hard and masculine, her legs,
her shoulders bent beneath the load
of children, her arms as big
as his and nearly as strong.

Who can keep them from the dust
gathering in corners, in cracks
between the wood, from darkness
growing in doorways, creeping
up every road they know

The old one is worn out
from too much labor, too little care,
too long a life like hers.

The years crawl through her fingers
wringing in pain, through her feet
swelling from constant standing.
The young one doesn't know any better,
thinks this is the only way,
will grow up hungry and happy,
his belly constantly sore.

There is only this one,
with eyes like caverns, a face
round as a question, legs
already scraped and scratched
but standing like none of the others,
a pillar between the walls,
between the doors and windows,
holding all that falls, apart.
There is only this one
I need to believe will make it.

Brock

It came as no surprise
that he'd die by a bullet,
that it'd be someone he knew,
someone with reasons he'd never
understand, the daughter he'd denied,
kept in closets, away from boys,
beneath the low roof, no windows,
dark heat, pictures of dead
uncles on the wall, dead and in the coffin,
dead and dressed like they never were,
eyes closed, hands folded
safe across their chests.

Everything had to be his way,
lined up, quiet, covered.
One day he kicked the dog so hard
for not getting out of his way
he broke two ribs and let her bleed
inside until his wife came home
to take her in. She growled at him
all the time after that
until he finally kicked her again.
That's when she knew he could do it
to her as well, when she left him
with his walls full of trophies,
his days without dissent.

They couldn't come to him to do it.
Somehow, in his own home,
he'd know before they could pull it off.

They had to lure him out
with something taken, something
that belonged to him.
She'd distract him with crying,
that always worked, then jump in the car
with him when he gave chase,
the second gun already in place.
He'd stop, get out, imagine himself
heroic, never see the bullet
fired from behind, never know
it wasn't about money at all.

Meta

Meta was the smart one, it seemed,
married money, at least by Riddle
standards, lived in a brick home
with two bathrooms, never worked
a day in her life except to volunteer
at church, keeping her handkerchief
at her mouth when meeting others,
believing the devil and disease rode
the same evil vapors, raised
her three girls to be moral,
upright and always safe.

She lost her oldest to rock music,
she always said, the devil's temptations
of lust and liquor, kicked her out
when she refused to return the Stones
album she'd bought with her own money
earned from babysitting and birthdays.

Her second was gone before she turned
fourteen with a boy three years older,
a fast car, a smooth tongue, and an urge
to start living before it was too late.

She threw the television out after that,
forbade all music but worship,
took her youngest out of school, taught her
everything she needed to know from the Bible
and Emily Post, made her the only
shadow visible behind her.

Willy Marie

As wide as she was tall,
as wide as her voice,
singing hymns, humming,
calling dogs, pigs, chickens,
as wide as any woman would need to be
on a farm on the other side
of Lake Greenwood, 10 miles
from the nearest intersection,
as wide as her name
Wilhelmina Marie Frances Elizabeth,
called after both grandmothers,
rare lapsed Catholics in the Upstate,
another 40 miles from the nearest Mass,
as wide as her initials, eight straight
strokes she sometimes joined into one
like mountains, 3 peaks, 3 valleys,
as wide as the smile she wore
every day of her life, even the bad days,
losing parents, grandparents, becoming
the last in a long line to own
2000 acres of corn and hogs,
even the day she understood
what it meant to be born
without a womb, rare genetic
occurrence, less common than
six fingers, conjoined twins.

Kendall

Ultimately, he had to shoot them both.
He had gone along when she took
him out of school at 10, had watched
them grow closer together as he became
unnecessary, someone only there
at night, taking up room in the bed.
He knew she could be strange
at times, often quiet, unmovable,
sometimes easy to fly to rage, never
quite satisfied with anything except the boy,
but he never imagined how far things had gone.

He had already knocked her down,
but she came at him again with the knife.
Despite the blood streaming from neck
and chest, he managed to crawl behind
the sofa, kick the table into her legs,
reach into the drawer she'd forgotten
in her rage and squeeze off two rounds
as she fell on top of him, the blade
slicing away half of his left ear.

He managed to punch the numbers on the phone
and lay waiting on the floor, a sofa pillow
pressed hard against his throat,
but the boy came home too soon
You'd think he might have seen the blood
pouring out of his father and had
at least a moment's doubt, but he left
the room running, screaming, "Murderer."

He knew where he was going, and he knew
he'd be back. He moved to the door,
one hand still holding the pillow
against his neck. He even got
the door open, but before he could close it
behind him, the bullet pierced his side,
came out the front and knocked him
to the ground, where another shattered his left
wrist before he fired two of his own,
one in the leg, one in the face
of the boy he could never love enough.

Jimmy Ligon

He got paid in eggs, corn, homemade pies
more often than cash, a rare commodity
in any amount among the farmers
around Lake Greenwood, too poor to afford
a town doctor for fixing legs, lancing
infections, stitching sides gored by horn
or spur. He rarely said anything about it,
thought his place was a dangerous one at best,
secured only by what he could do
and how many owed him. They'd arrive
before a cloud of dust, most telling
children to stay put, then returning
to the truck themselves to wait.
Those who let their kids play in the woods,
unafraid of black skin touching white,
he trusted just a bit more, laughed
at their jokes, extended a hand,
looked them in the eye. Dirt track
running down to woods and water's edge,
Old Man Garrison got plenty mad
when they paved it, put up that sign,
swore he'd never understand how the grandson
of a slave, his own daddy's slave
at that, could have a road named after him.
Most had always called it Ligon Road,
as long as there had been a road,
after the black man at the water end
on land his daddy had gotten a piece
at a time in trade for a lifetime

of fixing Garrison mules, a man
whose skills learned from father and grandfather
brought more traffic that way than two miles
and two hundred years of white-owned houses.

To

For weeks he'd hide pennies and quarters,
stockpile cokes and M & Ms,
tuck away toilet paper and underwear.
Some he'd keep beneath the bed,
rolled in tight wrappings of "The Beef People's"
brown paper bags. Others he'd stick
in knotholes of trees or cram, serious
as a squirrel, beneath the wellhouse eaves.

Then, at the exact hour, on the very day
he'd planned, with the map of everything he'd hidden
before him, he'd rise from the bed, tiptoe to the kitchen,
grab the dinner scraps to bribe the dogs
to silence, and slip through the door into darkness.

Seven times he ran away from home,
each time more certain he'd never look back.
Once he made it to the woods behind his Papa's farm,
once to the barn, once to the field's farthest corner.
One time he climbed a pine to the rooftop
and waited for morning's rescue to come.

Childhood was all the same series of leaving.
Eleven divorces between them. Three times
he watched his father leave, twelve brothers,
three sisters, two grandfathers, various uncles
and aunts, cousins beyond remembrance.
At 14 he decided he'd never leave.
At 17 he did.

Here is a man in love with high places,
with voices that say, "Jump. Step off.
Close your eyes and see if the wind
will lift you," who names the wind "hand
that moves moving, foot that walks
the floor of the sky, breath that whispers
to speak to roar." He has mastered the edible wild
and believes he has been a pair of legs forever.

He wants to know where it would get him
if, returning to the mountains, he'd find a doorway
in the sky. He remembers Cade's Cove
from his father and thinks he'd like to go there
when he's ready, to a bowl of land surrounded
by mountains, enough to try a different one
each day until he finds the one that will keep him.

Ed and His Brothers

"Been huntin'," they'd always say
while shaking his hand, their grins
revealing what they thought of anyone
who'd read Shakespeare, drove a minivan,
hadn't gone hunting since childhood.
He took it good-humoredly, sometimes
tossing a barb back, "Reviewed your portfolio?
Read Pinsky? Seen your kids?"

Then he'd listen to every story,
remember every point, never question
a claim, no matter how big or out of character.
He loved most to hear of creeks
and trees, trails that couldn't be followed
out again, animals who came so close
you could smell their musky wildness.

At the end of the day they'd each
go their own way, knowing next year
they'd meet again on common ground,
a white house, a forgotten world,
a place they would always call home.

Remembering Blue

Blue was always her favorite color,
cornflower and daisy, crocus and bouncingbet.
She remembers her mother's dishes, cobalt
blue glass. She remembers the ceiling
of the front porch summer afternoons,
lying back on the swing, roll of sky
captured in painted slats of blue. She made
a blue garden for shade, columbine,
iris, bellflower and forget-me-nots.
Even music they called the blues, lonely
and familiar, dripping like evening in her mind,
soft and slow and always a little bit sad.
Heaven for her would be like this,
a field full of flowers, ubiquity of blue.

Fallibility of Memory

This year the trees came
down, big bodies of pines
uprooted or cut off inches
from the ground. What started

as quarry noise, the low
rumbling behind the trees,
became the sounds of falling,
the fits of truck and dozer,

the spitting of chainsaws.
Through sudden gaps
childhood miles of dark woods
were laid bare, revealed

to be no more than a few thousand
feet from fence to quarry.
For days the trees fell
like limbs, not crashing,

like the giants they seemed
to be, but sliding slowly,
almost quietly, from limb
to limb until they landed

with dull thuds on blankets
of needles. They were wrapped
with chains and dragged to trucks
long with trees, their tracks

rutting red earth, smearing
deer trails across naked
slopes, stretching the creek
beyond its banks, spilling

its water into pools as deep
as graves. What was left
was piled in mounds to be
burned. Nothing was left

of memory, not the deer
stands, the tree house,
the forts of broom straw,
not the goat field, the fox

traps, the sliding rope,
not the battle-worn trails
that reached the end
of what we knew.

Compensation

We've filled the house with food again,
staved off another stubborn ghost of childhood,
starvation, uncertainty, neglect.
We drink, instead, our slow suicide
of whiskey and caffeine, suck
nicotine's faster poison,
pretend we've dealt with what remains
as if they were cards to be
distributed, picked up, arranged
into winning hands, my pair
bigger than yours, few things
better than a full house.

The Land Above This Line Is Oak and Hickory; Below Is Pine

From Thomas Anderson's 1817 Map of
South Carolina's Edgefield District

The difference between granite and clay
falling away to limestone, between trees
that break and those that bend out of the ground
roots and all, between stars blacked out
for half the year and those that shine year-round
faint but sure through yellow bristle of pine.
The difference between sandspur and beggar lice,
mistletoe and muscadine, plateau and sandhill
running out to plain, between names like Frogmore
and Clover, Soul's Harbor and Hard Labour Creek.

Each day they meet at the line like old friends,
shake hands above it, share the earth below.

Growing up along this line we knew that pine
meant climbing higher on limbs getting thinner
with each step upward, oak meant broad limbs
branching out from the same trunk, a cradle
you could hide in past nightfall.

This is a very specific place in every mind
it touches. It will be something you swung from,
something you crossed despite the danger of buckshot,
something you held tight before you,
your back bending against its going away.

In winter even the river stands up like a line.
It may now slide off the bed it has made

and not spread or fade into earth,
but splinter, shard, run like a great tongue
across your doorstep, dividing your house in half.

"Your house is sliding down the hill
and will soon be in the road," says one
to the other. "Yours is caving in
on itself and will be a pile of rubble
by next year." They depend on this.

"Died mostly of death," she says,
"like any day that won't last."

He spends his days counting, drawing lines
on maps frayed with rain. There is hardly a boundary
he hasn't crossed, though even he can't see
the lines he swears are there. The secret meaning
of the line is that it's made to be climbed
over, crawled under, walked around.

Stony Point

Crossroads where boulders rise
between Hodges and Ninety-Six,
Greenwood and Laurens, names
people might recognize, homage
to the quarry that kept three generations
of Garrisons, Harvleys, Duckworths,
microcosm of the American South,
Garrisons atop the hill, brick homes,
land left to woods or rented out,
worked by others, reaching
all the way back to the river,
managing schedules and paychecks,
sales and delivery, Harvleys half-way
down, wooden homes, on seven acres
they work to death for chickens and cows,
corn and the best tomatoes in three counties,
driving shovels and buckets, Duckworths
along the dusty road, a narrow strip
of land, two-room block homes
or later used trailers, drilling holes,
loading machines, setting charges
to break out proverbial hard places,
homes always half-empty.

First Peanut in America Grown Near This Site

from a marker near Waverly, VA

Not on this spot, you understand.
Not even in some primordial field
here lost to roads or billboards,
any such marker of community progress.
Not specifically north or south of here,
not exactly 1 mile, maybe 10,
roughly rounded to the nearest whole number.

Such wonderful vagueness makes anything possible.
Anyone standing on any inch of soil,
arms akimbo, might say, "Here it is,
the X of my body marking the very spot."
Or everyone for miles might claim
fame by association. Near here
Andrew Johnson was born, or James K. Polk,
George Washington slept, 22,000 died
in one day. Near here
Jack Johnson beat a white man,
King was killed or Kennedy or Garfield.
Near here Philip Freneau wrote
a poem, maybe leaning against this tree,
or that one, or one that looked like this one.
Near here a nation was destroyed,
men were hung, something or someone
great was conceived in the back of a Buick,
something else was given up as hopeless.

I felt power once when I stood
on the very spot Orville's wreck

left the ground. Now I wonder,
a barrier island, a dune of shifting sand.
Near here my uncle is buried.
Nearer he fired a shot somewhere
behind his left ear, his wife and daughter
nearby. The ground is nothing
like what they threw over him
as a preacher spoke his careful words
on a hot August day with sweat
dripping from each pallbearer's stony face.

At Lake Russell

Checking old maps I never find
Tucker's Ferry, Blackwell Bridge,
Trotter's Shoal, but the people
remember, and some among them
speak of older names too:
Tciloki, Yemassee, Creek.

The boy who left this country
never stopped hearing its names
echo in his ear. Coming home now
he can no longer follow the tracks
over water wider than he remembers,
find the field where he gathered blackberries,
built forts of broomstraw, the tree
where he watched for wild turkeys.
Walking banks he knew as woods
he points to spots on the lake,
says there I ran, there I climbed,
there I slid down red hills
to water waiting below.

Think of when the flood came:
the precious stones, opened flowers
buried beneath water, the trees shrinking
every day, lake rising to their knees,
waists, limbs: houses, bridges
left standing, streets running
quiet and crowded under water;
the land silenced, forbidden to speak
its own name, allowed only to say

what it knows of drowning.
When basements flooded they stayed
that way, dirt floors rising
to windows and doors left open in rain.

For weeks they came, to watch
the daily climb of water over banks
they fished from, fields they planted,
woods they knew like back yards.
Even now they come to hear names
that linger like river fog, like voices
carried over water from a distant boat,
to see what can grow from land
transformed to lake bed: dead trees,
river grass, bold stands of memory.

When you feel the past getting lost
behind you, like a road you can't
get back to, you can go there,
kneel down beside them, fill your hands
with water, raise it to the cup
of your ear, listen to names scratched
on headstones, left on mailboxes, carried
down country roads in mouths of old men,
listen to the years singing like crickets
their silvery song of memory.

The Exploration of Edges

I remember as a child expecting lines
on the ground separating North
Carolina from South, South Carolina
from Georgia, Greenwood County
from anywhere else. Often rivers
obliged, Catawba, Savannah, Saluda,
and one time in a place called Carowinds,
there it was, as I always expected
to see it, a broad, yellow stripe
saying, *Here you are one place;*
There you are somewhere else,
and of course I walked that line,
jumped from one side to the other,
stood with one foot on either side,
even lay across it, letting it slice
my body in two, head to the north,
everything below the waist more southerly,
but usually it was left to imagination.
There might be a sign—*Now Leaving*—
and then a thousand feet further—
Now Entering. I wondered how
they couldn't be on the same post
and thought I'd like to live
between the signs, not belonging
to anything except the earth.
Sometimes I'd close my eyes, picture
signs I'd seen on other roads and play
dot to dot in my mind, imagining
how the line was real enough
to split trees, slice mountains,

divide houses, loyalties, identities,
send neighbors to different schools,
create schizophrenics out of anything.
I wondered how I might change the line
by piling earth on top of it or how deep
I'd have to tunnel to get beneath it.
I came to know enough of atrophy
and erosion, tectonics and miscegenation,
to understand the necessity of neutral zones,
in places as thin as walls, in others,
off the tip of Argentina, for example,
where oceans meet, as wide as moving
water and every bit as tumultuous.

Reading the Weather

Hen's scratching and mare's tails
make tall ships carry low sails.

These are the simplest truths:

A backing wind says storms are nigh.
A veering wind will clear the sky.

to know the weather, read the weather;

Ring around the moon,
rain by noon.
Ring around the sun,
rain before night is done.

to know words, read words;

Summer fog will scorch a hog.

to know people, read people.

When grass is dry before morning light
    look for rain before the night.
When the dew is on the grass
    rain will never come to pass.

Nobody reads anymore,

Red sky at morning,
sailors take warning.
Red sky at night,
sailors delight.

waiting to be told by someone else

Birds roost before a storm.

what they themselves should tell.

Rails

Every child should have one, a pair, really,
a matched set, set apart just the right width
so that one foot pressed against each one
leaves you stretched out about as far
as you can go, unable to move, feeling
almost trapped, almost actually in danger.

And every child should walk them as if
that's what they were intended for,
leading out of town, around the curve,
along the river, revealing the backsides
of people's homes, clotheslines and refuse,
the yards you weren't supposed to see.

And every child should learn to balance
atop the railhead without the constant
unsightly tipping from side to side,
should be able to step exactly the distance
between the ties consistently, almost
marching without kicking up ballast.

And every child should have a bridge
they go under to hide and look
at dirty magazines and smoke cigarettes
and place coins on the rails to flatten
and see if this could be the one
to cause the train to leap the tracks.

And every child should know the lonely
distant sound of late night travel

when bad dreams have kept them awake
wondering where they come from, what
they bring or take, and where when it's all
done they might return and call home.

Last Supper in the Yellow Kitchen

One had to wonder what Jesus was doing
there in a kitchen so tight white walls
had turned to yellow from smoke and heat
and grease, but there he was, clueless
disciples beside him above the metal
table, red-rimmed, speckled, surrounded
by five wooden chairs with woven seats
and barely enough room to crawl in
between wall and table. He sat
every hour of every day,
palms and eyes upturned (caught
mid roll perhaps) above
bowls of grits and biscuit toast
and four boys with dirty faces,
overlooking a woman who never
sat at the table to eat, and men
who talked of nothing but farming and fishing.
Even years later, returning
long after the last time
anyone stayed for supper, to claim
what little remained, vintage bowl,
hen and rooster salt and pepper
shakers, I see him there, yellowing, otherwise
unchanged, silently waiting to ascend.

Homeplace

From that hill I could see
the asphalt plant choking the sky,
the girl scout camp beneath the pines
that echoed laughter on summer nights,
seven acres of red cows and corn,
the highway's red clay bank
leading the way to anywhere else.

Only in back the trees rose up,
a pine wall too thick to see
through, too tall to see over,
but quarry sounds kept imagination's
beasts alive and creeping closer.

Why should this be home,
a place I lived only between
other homes, once a year,
a month at a time at least till 12,
a place where evening sang with voices
of the old, the unambitious,
the not-too-distant wild,
a place where dying had its own season,
and everything smelled like dirt.

A place is just a place,
one as good or bad as the other.
It's the people you care for,
or hate, who keep you
coming back, or never let you go.

Acts of Defiance

Just a boy,
not yet eight,
and knowing nothing
of the world,
I simply did as I was told
and reached my hands,
my forearms, long and thin,
even up to the elbows,
into the bloody back end
of a moaning cow
to grasp what I felt there
and pull,
and pull harder
when it wouldn't come
until something appeared,
and pull harder still
until something became
a wet mess of calf
spilling into my lap
and my uncles laughing
and my grandfather,
his hand on my shoulder,
looking at me hard,
eyes full of seriousness
saying, *Good job.*
Good job.

A lifetime later,
at forty-one,
holding you

I finally understand
the weight of it all.
I look at your mother
spent in bed
and say, *Good job,*
and then into your own
uncomprehending eyes
and say again,
Good job.

Vacancy

The poems are all asleep now,
bedded down beneath their blanket
of exhaustion, mental fatigue,
satisfaction. No one lives here
anymore, the old man and woman
both gone, parents caught up
in other lives, children grown up,
married off, moved away.

The hill is still there, of course,
and one house still sits upon it,
the other become a part of the hill
itself. There are still pecan trees
and stray flowers, and new rocks
rising each winter, and the pines have regained
half their height, but the cows
belong to someone else now,
an absent renter, and no garden graces
the hillside, as if the land could only
be used and never again possessed.

Acknowledgments

Grateful acknowledgment is due the following journals in which some of these poems were previously published:

Amaranth Review: "Ghost House," "Skeleton," and
    "The Undiscovered Country"
Beloit Poetry Journal: "Between the Rails"
Carolina Literary Companion: "Reading the Weather"
Cold Mountain Review: "My Grandfather's Hands"
Cottonwood: "For One Who Knows How to Own Land"
Cream City Review: "To"
Dead Mule: "Dirt Farmer," "Rails," "Homeplace,"
    "Leaning through Darkness to See the Stars,"
    "Stony Point," and "Vacancy"
Flutter: "Remembering Blue"
Greensboro Review: "The Fallibility of Memory"
Heavy Bear: "Kendall"
Innisfree Poetry Review: "The Land Above This Line is
    Oak and Hickory; Below Is Pine" and "Acts of Defiance"
Luciole Press: "To Resist Fading"
Mind in Motion: "Rosemary Is: Remembrance"
Now and Then: "Carcasses"
Oak Bend Review: "Moccasins"
Ouroboros Review: "Willy Marie"
Overtures: "Feeding Time"
Owen Wister Review: "Now"
Panhandler: "All Summer Long the Rain"
    and "Coming to the Surface"
Pembroke: "Dowry" and "Slaughter"
Phase & Cycle: "Fixing the Lines"
Poet & Critic: "Breakings"

Poets & Poems: "Last Supper in the Yellow Kitchen"
Radiant Turnstile: "Buzzard"
Red Dirt Review: "Brock," "Ed and His Brothers," "Meta,"
    "My Granny's House," and "Triptych"
Rusty Truck: "7 Haiku: wildflowers; grandfather; and yellow"
    and "First Peanut in America Grown Near This Site"
Scythe: "The Exploration of Edges"
Side Stream: "Compensation"
Sketchbook: "7 Haiku: screen door"
Slow Dancer: "What Comes Next"
The Smoking Poet: "Jimmy Ligon"
Southern Poetry Review: "The Event Rightfully Remembered"
    and "Preserving the Horn"
Sow's Ear: "Holding On"
Sun Dog: "At Lake Russell"
Wellspring: "Driving Home from the Hospital"
Word Salad: "Regret"

*Cover photo, "The Fallibility of Memory" (from
the poem by Scott Owens), by Clayton Joe Young
(joeyoungphoto.com)*

*Cover design, photo effects, and book design by
Diane Kistner (dkistner@futurecycle.org)*

*Text type: Bookman Old Style with Candara
and 5AM Gender titling*

About FutureCycle Press

We are a small independent publisher dedicated to preserving for posterity the work of some of the best poets and flash fiction authors writing today. Our books, chapbooks, and anthologies are sold globally in paperback and digital ("ebook") formats on Amazon, through multiple distributors and resellers, and from our web site. For submission guidelines and additional information, visit us at www.futurecycle.org.

Poetry Books

Bullets in the Jewelry Box by Amy Riddell
For One Who Knows How to Own Land by Scott Owens
Air Swimmer by Robert W. Kimsey
Mosslight by Kimberley Pittman-Schulz
Leave It Behind by Emily Raabe
Stealing Hymnals from the Choir by Timothy Martin
Castaway by Katherine Riegel
Simple Weight by Tania Runyan
Luminous Dream by Wally Swist
No Loneliness by Temple Cone
Beyond the Bones by Neil Carpathios
Violet Transparent by Anne Coray
The Porous Desert by David Chorlton

Poetry Chapbooks

Scything by Joanne Lowery
A Love Letter to Say There Is No Love
by Maria Williams-Russell
The Secret Life of Hardware by Cheryl Lachowski
Colma by John Laue

www.ingramcontent.com/pod-product-compliance
Lightning Source LLC
Chambersburg PA
CBHW070002100426
42741CB00012B/3102